The Groundhog Day Book
of Facts and Fun

BY Wendie Old

ILLUSTRATED BY Paige Billin-Frye

Albert Whitman & Company, Morton Grove, Illinois

For Ariana and Willow.—W. O.

For my grandmother, Gertrude Barmore Billin.—P. B.-F.

Library of Congress Cataloging-in-Publication Data

Old, Wendie C.
The Groundhog Day book of facts and fun / by Wendie C. Old ; illustrated by Paige Billin-Frye.
p. cm.
ISBN 0-8075-3066-2 (hardcover)
1. Groundhog Day. I. Billin-Frye, Paige. II. Title.
GT4995.G76.O53 2004   394.261—dc22   2004000523

The design is by Carol Gildar.

For more information about Albert Whitman & Company, please visit our web site at www.albertwhitman.com.

Riddles by:
Elaine Marie Alphin (p. 40, "crowned hog"); Jo Ellen Bogart (p. 40, "poundhog"); Susan Taylor Brown (p. 29, p. 40, "Frankenstein monster");
Marianne Dyson (p. 11); Debbie Gibbons (p. 18); Abby Levine (p. 40, "groundhog's laundry," "favorite food,"
"how do groundhogs smell?" "sick groundhogs"); Currien MacDonald (pp. 8, 23);
Dian Curtis Regan (p. 40, "roundhog"); April Pulley Sayre (p. 33); Jane Yolen (p. 30, top).

Acknowledgments

I am grateful to Dr. Stam Zervanos of Pennsylvania State University/Berks, who double-checked groundhog facts and also provided interesting, up-to-date information about groundhogs from his own research.

Thanks to all my internet friends who invented riddles for this book. And to Rick Walton, who taught me how to create jokes and riddles. And finally, thanks to Paige Billin-Frye, whose illustrations bring life to every page. —W.O.

CONTENTS

Chapter 1
The Groundhog Sees Its Shadow—or Not

Will the groundhog see its shadow? That is the question each year on February 2nd. Almost everyone in the United States waits for the news from Punxsutawney (PUNGK-suh-taw-nee), a little town in the mountains of western Pennsylvania.

If a groundhog named Punxsutawney Phil sees his shadow, there will be six more weeks of winter. If he does not see his shadow, spring will come early.

The temperature on February 2nd in western Pennsylvania is usually below freezing. Almost always, snow covers the ground. And still, more than five thousand people gather on Gobbler's Knob—a hill outside Punxsutawney.

The gate in the fence around Gobbler's Knob opens at three o'clock in the morning. People rush in to find a good spot on the wooded hillside near the stage. Soon the hillside is alive with lights, music, and dancing.

Other groundhogs predict the weather, too.

At six-thirty, fireworks explode over the hill. By seven o'clock, men in top hats and long, dark coats gather on the stage at the top of the hill. These are members of the Inner Circle of the Punxsutawney Groundhog Club. Special guests from all over the world find their places close by. The music stops. The crowd hushes.

On the stage sits a tall fake tree stump. At seven-twenty-five, the Groundhog Handler reaches into the stump. His thick gloves are not only for warmth. They're also protection against the sleepy

What's green, has four legs, and jumps out of its hole on February 2nd?

The Ground Frog!

groundhog accidentally biting or scratching him.

He pulls out Punxsutawney Phil, "King of the Groundhogs, Seer of Seers, Sage of Sages, Prognosticator of Prognosticators, and Weather Prophet Extraordinary." He holds the groundhog high so everyone can see him. The crowd cheers.

Then he allows Phil time to look for his shadow. The Groundhog Club president leans toward the groundhog to hear his verdict. Phil whispers into the president's ear. He, of course, speaks in "groundhogeese," but the president understands this language.

What does Phil say? Possible poetic predictions have already been written on scrolls. These scrolls are lying in piles close to Phil's fake burrow.

Phil tells the president to choose the poem that most exactly fits his weather prediction. This poem is read to the crowd in a loud, dramatic manner. Television, radio, newspaper, and internet reporters send the word to the whole world. The crowd on Gobbler's Knob cheers again. (The crowd would cheer no matter what Phil predicted. They're just there to have fun.) Music blasts out over the hill. Dancing and celebration go on throughout the day.

Over forty thousand people visit Punxsutawney during this festival. On the days before and after Groundhog Day, they join in all sorts of activities featuring groundhogs. Groundhog Festival flags line the streets of Punxsutawney, and a huge groundhog statue welcomes visitors to town.

These weather predictions have been coming from Punxsutawney for over a hundred years. In the 1880s, Clymer H. Freas, city editor of the *Punxsutawney Spirit* newspaper, began writing newspaper stories about a group of local men who hunted and barbecued groundhogs. He called the hunters the Punxsutawney Groundhog Club.

One of his stories concerned the tradition of groundhogs predicting whether spring would be early or late. He and other members of the group even created a name for a groundhog—Punxsutawney Phil.

The first prediction was published on February 2, 1886. "Today is groundhog day and up to the time of going to press the beast has not seen its shadow." The report of the first trip to Gobbler's Knob was made the following year. The ceremony itself was held in secret until 1966. Only Phil's prediction was announced to the public. Over the years, W. O. Smith, the owner of the *Punxsutawney Spirit* (who was also a United States Congressman), worked hard at keeping the legend alive.

Every few years, the animal making the predictions grew old and died, but his young replacement was always called by the same name. In time, because of all the publicity in Congress and elsewhere, Phil became the semi-official weather forecaster for the nation.

Chapter 2
The Reason for Seasons

The seasons make a circle—from January to December and on to January again—from winter to spring to summer to fall to winter. (The closer you get to the equator, the more the seasons simply change from wet to dry. And the temperature hardly changes at all.)

Circles.

Why?

Because our planet Earth orbits (goes around) the Sun.

Imagine a line drawn through the north and south poles of the earth. This is the planet Earth's axis. Earth spins around this axis once every twenty-four hours. When one side of the planet faces the Sun, it has daytime. As the earth turns, that side will face away from the Sun. Now it is dark—nighttime.

The axis is not vertical (straight up and down) in relation to the Sun, but is tilted. It is because the earth is tilted as it orbits the Sun that we have different seasons.

Each orbit takes one year. As the earth moves around the Sun, for six months the Northern Hemisphere (northern half) of the earth, where the United States is located, tilts toward the Sun. The Sun's rays hit the Northern Hemisphere straight on and warm it.

What do lunar groundhogs do on February 2nd?

Whatever they want. There are no seasons on the moon.

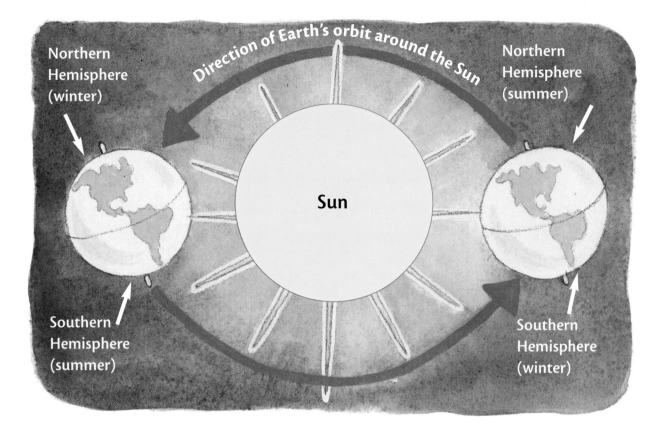

For the other six months, the Southern Hemisphere (southern half of the earth) is tilted toward the Sun and the Northern Hemisphere is tilted away. The Sun's rays strike the Northern Hemisphere at an angle; they are not strong or direct.

At the North Pole and the South Pole, the weather is almost always cold. These areas always get the least amount of sunshine, no matter what the season.

From about March 21 to about September 22, more of the Northern than the Southern Hemisphere faces toward and is warmed by the Sun. We have spring and summer. This is reversed from September to March, when the Southern Hemisphere gets more sun, and the Northern Hemisphere has fall and winter.

Winter is a hard time for animals and people. It is cold. Food is scarce for wild animals. There is more darkness than daylight. Bad weather often keeps people trapped indoors for days. Some people become depressed and sad. Many animals cope with the cold and scarcity of food by sleeping more during the winter.

Spring is a time of rebirth. Flowers bloom—even in the desert of the American Southwest. Birds and animals are born. Grass and other plants that have looked dead all winter now show signs of green life.

It's only natural that humans would look for signs to forecast the end of cold weather or drought and the beginnings of new life again.

Chapter 3
Deep in the Earth

What is a groundhog?

What is a woodchuck?

What is a whistle pig?

What is a marmot?

Actually, groundhogs are woodchucks are whistle pigs are marmots. These are all different names for the same small furry beast. Groundhogs can be found in the eastern woodlands in the United States, in Canada, and as far west as parts of Alaska. They are a kind of marmot, which is a member of the ground squirrel family.

The name woodchuck comes from a Native American word. In the Algonquin language (used by many tribes in Canada and the United States), groundhogs were called *wojak.* European settlers pronounced it "woodchuck." The name whistle pig comes from the shrill sound these animals make when warning each other of danger.

Most woodchucks or groundhogs are about twenty inches long, weighing from five to ten pounds. They waddle around like tubby ducks on their short legs. Their fur is brown, rough, and shaggy with flecks of white at the tips. They have short, stubby tails. They live mostly underground

What side of the groundhog has the most hair?

The outside..

and hibernate each winter from about November to March.

Like rats, mice, squirrels, and beavers, groundhogs are rodents. Rodents have two large upper front teeth for gnawing woody stems of plants. They also like softer foods such as leaves, clover, flowers, and berries. All this chewing wears their teeth down. However, as long as rodents live, their teeth keep growing to replace the worn-off parts.

Groundhogs are the major hole-digging animal in the eastern United States. They live in homes called burrows that they dig in the ground. Their curved front claws tear through the earth. Their flat heads push the dirt aside, and their back feet toss the dirt behind them. Their sharp teeth chew through any tree or plant root that gets in the way.

Each burrow has several tunnels leading to the surface. These tunnels can often reach thirty feet long and be as much as six feet below ground. About seven hundred pounds of dirt can be pushed out by a groundhog digging a thirty-foot tunnel! All this digging is good for the soil, exposing subsoil and helping to turn it into topsoil.

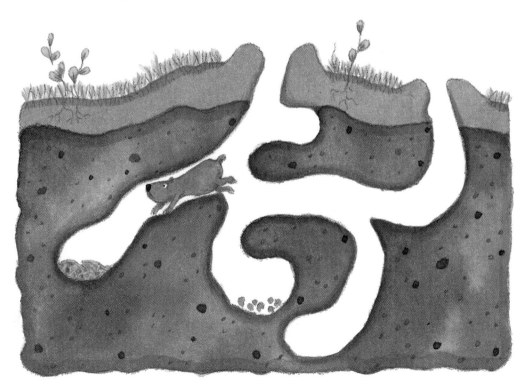

Where does all that dirt go? It gets shoved out the front door. Most of it is scattered by rain and wind. Some of it stays close by, making a mound that hides the entrance. The mound is a great spot for the groundhog to sit and watch for enemies. The side exits are also hidden.

Inside the burrow, the tunnels connect several rooms. These rooms can be used for sleeping or storing bits of snack food. One room can be used as a toilet.

When they are away from their burrows, groundhogs will often stop eating to sit up, with their front paws tucked high on their chests, making themselves tall to watch for danger. At the first sign, they give their piercing whistle sound to warn other groundhogs in the area. Quick! Scatter! Run! Scurry into tall grass or into the burrow to hide!

A groundhog will always try to be close to one of the entrances. This way it can quickly dive into the hole and escape anything that tries to catch and eat it.

Foxes, wolves, bobcats, and some large birds such as eagles, hawks, and owls hunt groundhogs. Sometimes people do, too. That's because groundhogs enjoy fresh green vegetables—just like people. If they are nesting near farms or gardens, they will eat crops.

Usually groundhogs live alone. Males and females do not share burrows. Females care for their young during the spring and summer, encouraging them to eat and grow fat. Then, as fall approaches, the young leave their mother to find or dig their own burrows. The females stay close to their home burrow, but the males travel farther away.

In the winter, the groundhog hibernates in the deepest room in its burrow, with only one entrance, for safety. It will make a plug to stop up

What is a groundhog's favorite book?

HOLES by Louis Sachar.

Holes

the entrance to its sleeping area and to keep cold air out. Some groundhogs have two dens—one for the summer and the other for hibernation.

Hibernation is a deep sleep. When the groundhog hibernates, its body temperature drops to around 40 degrees. That's about the temperature in your refrigerator. It doesn't freeze solid, however, because it makes sure that its sleeping den is below the frost line in the ground.

(During below-freezing weather, even the ground becomes frozen—sometimes to a depth of two feet. Below that, the earth is cold, but not frozen. The point where the earth stops being frozen is called the frost line.)

To survive hibernation, groundhogs must get very fat. Starting at the end of summer, they stuff themselves with food. This makes them so tubby that when cold weather arrives, they can hardly walk. In the fall, the shorter days, colder temperatures, and a lack of food turn on the groundhogs' hibernation mechanism (scientists are not yet sure how this mechanism works), and they fall into a deep sleep.

While they hibernate, curled in a tight ball, groundhogs live off their body fat. They don't need to wake up to eat. However, they do rouse ten to fifteen times over the winter, for periods ranging from an hour to a day. Then they go back to sleep. When they wake, they might go to the bathroom in a nearby room.

No matter the season, groundhogs wake about seven A.M., though there is no cue to time in their deep, dark burrows. Even when they rouse during hibernation, they still wake at seven. This is because something in their brain acts like a clock to wake them at the same time each morning.

During hibernation, all of the groundhogs' body functions slow down. Their heartbeats slow from about ninety beats a minute to anywhere from thirty to fifty. The colder they get, the slower their hearts beat. They breathe only every five or six minutes. Even their teeth stop growing. However, despite using just a tiny bit of energy to live, they can burn up a third of their body weight over the winter.

Groundhogs hibernate from ninety to one hundred sixty days, depending on where they live (hibernation begins as early as September in colder areas). Then their internal clock tells them it is time to wake up. As they wake, they begin to feel the cold. They shiver. Groundhogs have a special brown fat lying across the back and shoulders, close to the brain and liver. It is not used as food during the winter. Shivering tells the brown fat to create heat, bringing the groundhogs' body temperature up to normal.

While the groundhog is sleeping far underground, other animals, such as rabbits, might use its tunnel exits for winter nests. Abandoned groundhog burrows are also used as homes by rabbits, snakes, raccoons, and foxes. Nothing gets wasted in nature.

What do you have when you cross a groundhog with a peanut?

An animal who predicts spring and acts like a nut!

Chapter 4
Do Groundhogs Really Wake Up in February?

Like other groundhogs, Punxsutawney Phil hibernates during the winter. Right before February 2nd, Groundhog Day, Phil is put in a burrow underneath the fake tree stump on the stage on top of Gobbler's Knob. This burrow is electrically heated. The heat wakes Phil from his hibernation sleep in time to make his prediction.

What should you do if you find a groundhog sleeping in your bed?

Sleep somewhere else.

But scientists have discovered that many hibernating wild animals, such as hedgehogs, badgers, bears, and groundhogs, really do wake up naturally in late January or early February, even though winter might last for six more weeks. One scientist is Dr. Stam Zervanos, who teaches biology at Pennsylvania State University. Since 1999, he has observed the thirty-two groundhogs living on a university experimental farm.

He monitors them, fifteen at a time. He puts hidden cameras outside their burrows and checks their movements with small transmitters placed under their skin. A computer system automatically scans the animals every hour and records their locations and body temperatures. Zervanos can even place transmitters in burrows to find the temperature there. He catches a groundhog in a cage trap, ties a transmitter to its tail, and once the groundhog is back in its burrow, he pulls the string and the transmitter falls to the ground!

All of Zervanos's groundhogs go into hibernation by the beginning of November. By late January/early February, most of them have come out of their dens.

What kinds of stories do baby groundhogs like best at bedtime?

Furry Tales.

The males roam the area, exploring. The females stay near the openings of their burrows. It seems as if the males are checking out the females, looking for sweethearts. And if a female likes a male, she invites him to come visit for a while, deep in her winter den.

This waking up and roaming seems to be a part of the groundhogs' mating ritual. They probably don't mate at this time. But it may be necessary for these animals, who usually live alone, to simply get to know each other. Then they go back to their own burrows to sleep until March, when they wake up for good and mate.

If they were to mate in early February, when they first wake, it would be too soon. The babies would be born too early, in March, when there is very little growing yet for them to eat. If the babies are born too late, in June, they will not be able to grow big and store enough fat to survive hibernation in the wintertime. Only babies created during the first two weeks in March will survive to live a normal three-to-five-year lifespan.

Chapter 5
The Beginnings of Groundhog Day

Many civilizations have spring festivals. Festivals that celebrate the end of the cold time (or the dry time) and the beginning of the warmer weather (or rains). The time of birth and growth.

During the first years of our calendar, people in the Roman Empire celebrated a spring festival in early February. On this day they cleaned their houses and farmyards. They used special rites to purify themselves and their homes.

At the same time in ancient Ireland, people called the Celts (KELTS) had a religious celebration called Imbolc (IM-bolk). This celebration came halfway between the winter solstice (about December 21—the shortest day of the year) and the spring equinox (about March 21, when day and night are the same length). It was celebrated on February 1st or 2nd.

Celebrations of the halfway points between the winter or summer solstices and spring or fall equinoxes have been held for centuries. Imbolc and Groundhog Day are among them. Halloween or All Souls' Day (or Day of the Dead) are others. Two other halfway

What happens if the ground log sees its shadow?
We'll have six more weeks of splinters!

points are May Day on May 1st, and Lammas, a harvest celebration on August 1st formerly celebrated in England.

Imbolc was dedicated to Brigit, the Celtic goddess of poetry, home crafts, fire, fertility, and healing. The Celtic people believed she prepared the way for springtime. To symbolize spring's arrival, the fire that had been burning all winter in the fireplace was put out. The hearth was cleaned, the house swept, and new fires built.

By the middle of the fifth century A.D., the day was observed as the feast day of the Christian saint Brigit. The first signs of spring arrive in many places, including Ireland, around St. Brigit's Day. Lambs are born and grass begins to grow again.

On February 2nd, St. Brigit's Day, many people marched in a procession in church holding lit candles. During the church service, which was called a mass, the priest blessed these candles. That evening, these blessed candles glowed in each window of homes to ward off the darkness of winter and encourage spring to come. This may have been a substitution for the older tradition of rekindling the hearth fire.

The day became known as Candlemas. People believed that the weather on Candlemas would predict the weather for the next six weeks.

A British Candlemas verse says,

> *If Candlemas be fair and bright,*
> *winter has another flight.*
> *If Candlemas brings clouds and rain,*
> *winter will not come again.*

An old Scottish verse says,

> *If Candlemas Day is bright and clear,*
> *there'll be two winters in the year.*

Nobody knows how it started, but gradually legends grew that if an animal came out of hibernation on Candlemas and saw its shadow, winter would last six more weeks. An old German saying is,

> *When the bear sees his shadow at Candlemas,*
> *he will crawl back into his hole for another six weeks.*

But how did a sunny day—when an animal can cast a shadow—come to mean that winter would last six more weeks? You would expect a sunny day to mean that spring was on the way.

How do you ask a 4,000-pound groundhog to move out of your way?

Very politely!

Perhaps it is because in February sunny days are cold and dry. Warmer days have more moisture in the air, causing clouds—and no shadows. So if a groundhog sees its shadow, the day is probably sunny and cold. If it's cold, there may be six more weeks of winter.

People in Germany thought that it might be a bear or badger who watched for its shadow on Candlemas. Traditions in other European countries included hedgehogs as weather predictors. In all cases, it is a hibernating animal that is checking to see if spring will arrive soon.

Germans who settled in Pennsylvania in the mid-eighteenth century brought the Candlemas tradition with them. They found few badgers and no hedgehogs in this area. (And bears are not easy to find. Anyway, it's best to stay away from cranky, hungry bears in the springtime!) However, many groundhogs live in Pennsylvania. It was logical to give the job of predicting spring weather to the groundhog.

The earliest reference to Groundhog Day in North America is in James Morris's diary for February 4, 1841. He was a storekeeper in Morgantown, Pennsylvania. Morris wrote:

> *Last Tuesday, the 2nd, was Candlemas day, the day on which, according to the Germans, the Groundhog peeps out of his winter quarters and if he sees his shadow he pops back for another six weeks nap, but if the day be cloudy he remains out, as the weather is to be moderate.*

Chapter 6
More Than Punxsutawney Phil?

Is Punxsutawney Phil the one, the only, Seer of Seers, the Weather Prognosticator to the World? Not really. There are others.

Wiarton Willie, in Ontario, Canada, is an albino groundhog. (Albino animals have no pigment, or color, in their skin, hair, or eyes. Their fur or skin is white or pale; their eyes look pink or light blue.)

For many years Wiarton Willie predicted the spring weather for eastern Canada. However, in 1999, when the townspeople went to dig him out of hibernation, he was dead.

What a disaster! The town of Wiarton was in the midst of its usual huge celebration of the day—and was full of tourists and journalists. What could the townspeople do?

They tried to pass off a stuffed groundhog as the actual one.

That didn't work.

They put out a call for another Willie. He had to be an albino groundhog. Two young white groundhogs were found. Now Wiarton has two albino groundhogs. Both of them are called Wee Willie.

Groundhog Day has become so popular in North America that many places have set up their own groundhogs to forecast the spring weather. Here are some other Weather Prognosticators:

Gen. Beauregard Lee—Official Weather Prognosticator for the state of Georgia. He lives on the Yellow River Game Ranch near Lilburn, Georgia, in a miniature Southern mansion called "Weathering Heights." He is lured out with a bowl of hash browns.

Who leaps tall buildings with a single bound?

Superhog!

Shubenacadie Sam—the Shubenacadie Wildlife Park's local meteorologist in Nova Scotia, Canada.

Octorara Orphie—of Quarryville, Pennsylvania. In Quarryville, Groundhog Sighting Squads are dispatched to observe live groundhogs in the woods and consult with them about the weather.

Ridge Lea Larry—a stuffed groundhog in the Geology Department of the State University of New York at Buffalo.

Staten Island Chuck—a groundhog at the Staten Island Zoo gives the official Groundhog Day forecast for that part of New York. The zoo offers juice, coffee, and bagels for those who brave the cold in hopes of learning about an early spring.

There are also Buckeye Chuck from Marion, Ohio; Pothole Pete in New York City; Sir Walter Wally of Raleigh, North Carolina; Pierre C. Shadeaux in New Iberia, Louisiana; Jimmy the Groundhog from Sun Prairie, Wisconsin; and many more.

What is a laughing groundhog called?

A grinhog.

How can you tell a groundhog from a duck?

You can't tell a groundhog anything. They only understand groundhogeese.

Some towns don't use groundhogs to predict the coming of spring. Vancouver, British Columbia, Canada, has Furby the Wonder Chicken. Furby insists she is a ground chicken, not a groundhog.

Indianapolis, Indiana, used to have a groundhog named Henrietta. But in 1993 her job was taken over by a hedgehog named Hilary.

The Lions Club of Cottage Grove, Wisconsin, uses Hamlet the Potbellied Pig.

There is even a "virtual" groundhog in Bonn, Germany. It has to be an internet virtual groundhog because real groundhogs do not live in Europe. They only live in North America.

Chapter 7
Six More Weeks of Winter?

Can groundhogs predict the weather?

Punxsutawney residents insist that their groundhog, Phil, has never been wrong in over one hundred years. However, the United States National Oceanic and Atmospheric Administration (NOAA) did a study in 2001 and found that Phil had been right only one out of three times.

Wiarton Willie's prediction rate for Canada is just as bad. David Phillips, a climatologist at Environment Canada, found that groundhogs are right only 36 percent of the time. (Only a little more than one out of three times.)

If the groundhog sees its shadow, it is supposed to mean there will be six more weeks of winter. If it does not see its shadow, this means spring is just around the corner. Almost 90 percent of the time, Phil sees his shadow. If his forecast was always accurate, this should mean spring would be late 90 percent of the time. It isn't.

Punxsutawney Phil's prediction is only correct one-third of the time. Therefore, the only thing Phil is announcing is that the weather is more often sunny than cloudy in Punxsutawney, Pennsylvania, in early February.

What does a groundhog call his father's father?

Grandhog.

It doesn't seem to have anything to do with how soon spring will actually arrive and stay.

But celebrating Groundhog Day is a fun thing to do. And it doesn't hurt to hope for an early spring and the end of cold weather.

In the year 2003 on February 2nd, the temperature was 33 degrees above zero Fahrenheit (one degree above freezing). Phil saw his shadow.

That year, spring arrived late.

Hey—he was right!

Chapter 8
Have a Groundhog Day Party!

INVITATION:

Supplies:
Brown construction paper and another color paper, or white paper
Scissors, glue, pen

You could buy invitations from a card store, or you can make your own. Using the pattern here, cut groundhogs out of brown construction paper, making sure that you have the fold of the paper along the left-hand side of the groundhog.

The groundhog should be no taller than 5 inches and no wider than 3 inches so that it will fit into a regular envelope.

Inside the groundhog card, glue the invitation, which should be on either another color of construction paper or on white paper. The invitation should include this information:

You're Invited to a Groundhog Day Party!

At:_____

Time :_____

Date :_____

Please call: _____
              (your name)

Tel. #: _____

And *let* us know if you can
or cannot come.

fold

You're Invited to a Groundhog Day Party!

(front)

(inside)

GAMES:

Get the Groundhog Back into Its Burrow:

Supplies:
A ball (brown, if possible) or beanbag
A trash can, box, or some receptacle with holes cut in it
Masking tape to mark the distance away from the burrow

Stand at the tape and toss the beanbag or ball toward the burrow.
Each person gets three chances to send the groundhog home.
This can also be done with teams.

Hot Groundhog

Supplies:
A soft stuffed groundhog toy, a puppet, or a brown beanbag
A tape or CD with music and a tape or CD player

Sit in a circle. Someone starts the music. As it plays, pass the groundhog around the circle, acting as if the animal is hot and must be passed along quickly.

Someone stops the music. Whoever is holding the groundhog is out.
Continue playing until only one person is left.

SHADOWS:

First, talk about Groundhog Day and shadows. (Things that get in the way of the sun or a bright light cause shadows.)

There are lots of activities you can do with shadows.

1. Shadow Tag

If it is sunny outside and it is early or late enough for your body to cast shadows, play shadow tag. Instead of touching a person, whoever is "It" must run and step on someone's shadow.

2. Shadow Art

Supplies:
A large flashlight or other source of light
A roll of newsprint or large pieces of white paper

For each child, tape a piece of paper to the wall.

If the paper is small, have a child sit on a chair while another child (or an adult helper) draws the shadow of his or her head or hand on the paper.

If the paper is large enough, have a child stand in front of it while another child (or adult helper) draws his or her whole shadow on the paper.

Put names on the back of the paper.

Then have a display of shadows and let everyone guess whose shadow is whose.

3. Shadow Fun

You could also make big shadows, little shadows, animal shadows, and moving shadows.

4. Guess the Shadow

Fill a bag with lots of solid objects with simple shapes such as a paintbrush, scissors, a crayon, a pencil, a small car, a spoon, a piece of a puzzle, a toothbrush, a small book, etc. Everyone must guess what the thing is from the shape of the shadow it makes. Take turns picking objects for the others to guess.

5. Shadows and Seasons

Supplies:
A ball that looks like our planet Earth or an actual globe.
A flashlight or other source of strong light

If using a ball, mark it to show the hemispheres and the general outline of the continents.

One person stands in the middle of the room, shining the flashlight on the "earth." (The person holding the "earth" must make sure that the tilt is correct for our Earth.)

The person holding the earth moves in a circle around the Sun (flashlight). (Make sure the Sun always turns to shine on the earth.)

This should show how (on one side of the room), the Sun shines more strongly on the Northern Hemisphere, and how (on the other side of the room), the Sun shines more strongly on the Southern Hemisphere.

A CRAFT TO MAKE:
. . . .

Pop-up Groundhogs

Supplies:
Glue
A cup (foam or paper, not waxed), or toilet paper rolls
Sand or brown or green construction paper or felt
Craft sticks or popsicle sticks
Brown pompoms (3/4 or 1 inch)

Tiny brown pompoms (optional for ears)
1/4-inch wiggle eyes
Shredded brown paper (paper bags)

Take the cup and cover the outside with glue.

Roll it in sand or cover with brown ("dirt") or green ("grass") construction paper or felt.

Take a stick. Glue the large brown pompom on one end for the groundhog's head.

Glue on two small brown pompoms for ears (optional).

Glue on wiggly eyes.

Make a small slit in the bottom of the cup.

Press the free end of the stick through the slot.

Press shredded brown paper into the cup around the groundhog.

Move the stick up and down to make the groundhog look out of its burrow to see its shadow.

An alternate burrow could be an empty toilet paper roll.

FOOD:

Many types of snacks would be fun to eat at this party:

1. A mix of cereals, nuts, and raisins that looks like possible groundhog food.

2. Since groundhogs eat plants, serve a platter of sliced vegetables

3. A cake could have a groundhog picture on it. Many bakeries will make one. Or an adult could help you make the picture yourself.

4. You could decorate chocolate cupcakes with icing to resemble groundhogs. (This could be a group project.)

5. Or you could have a large chocolate cake with chocolate buttercream icing and chocolate sprinkles on it to look like a groundhog's furry body. Take the pompom groundhog head on a stick you created and insert the stick into the cake.

CLOSING ACTIVITY:

Will spring be early or will spring be late? Write down your prediction.

In six weeks, look at your prediction to see if you were right.

HAPPY GROUNDHOG DAY!

More Groundhog Riddles

What do you call a groundhog's laundry?
Hogwash.

How do groundhogs smell?
With their noses.

What's a groundhog's favorite food?
Burrow-itos.

Where do sick groundhogs go?
To the hogpital.

What do you get if you cross
Frankenstein's monster with a
groundhog?
I don't know, but I'm not sticking
around to find out.

What do you call a groundhog adopted
from the Humane Society?
A poundhog.

What do you call a groundhog who eats too much?
A roundhog.

What do you call a royal groundhog?
A crowned hog.